DISCOVER

THE BIBLE

THROUGH RHYME

Snapshots of Each Book of the Bible

Jerilyn Allen

Inset Illustrations by Jerilyn Allen

Copyright © 2021 by Jerilyn Allen

Cover Design: istockphoto.com
Illustrations from istockphoto.com

All rights reserved. This book or any portion thereof may not be reproduced or used in any manner whatsoever without the express written permission of the author except for the use of brief quotations in a book review.

All Scripture quotations, unless otherwise noted, are taken from the New American Standard Bible
The Lockman Foundation
1960, 1962, 1968, 1971, 1972, 1973,
A Corporation Not for Profit
La Habra, California
Producers of the Amplified Translations
All rights reserved.

Verses marked NKJV are taken from the New King James Version®.
Copyright © 1982 by Thomas Nelson. Used by permission.
All rights reserved.

Painted Gate Publishing
ISBN 978-1-952465-19-2

Dedication

To Believers and Unbelievers

I believe it is critical in this day and age for those who *claim* to be believers in Christ, to get to know this person Who died for them.

My prayer for those who don't know the Word of God is to pique their interest in this easy, fun way, and hopefully encourage them to seek all of God's Word, with all of their heart, and all of their mind, and all of their strength and all of their soul.

The time has come to know and stand for God and His Word.

With this book, I humbly attempt to glorify God.

The entrance of Your words gives light;
It gives understanding to the simple.
Psalm 119:130 (NKJV)

TABLE OF CONTENTS

OLD TESTAMENT
Genesis……………………………….. 4
Exodus…………………………….... 7
Leviticus…………………………….. 8
Numbers…………………………… 9
Deuteronomy……………………….10
Joshua…………………………….. 11
Judges……………………………….12
Ruth………………………………….13
I Samuel……………………………. 14
II Samuel…………………………….15
I & II Kings………………………….16
I & II Chronicles……………………17
Ezra………………………………….18
Nehemiah…………………………...19
Esther……………………………….20
Job………………………………….. 21
Psalms……………………………….23
Proverbs…………………………….24
Ecclesiastes………………………….25
Song of Solomon……………………..26
Isaiah……………………………….27
Jeremiah……………………………. 28
Lamentations……………………… 29
Ezekiel……………………………….30
Daniel……………………………….32

Hosea 33
Joel 34
Amos 35
Obadiah 37
Jonah 39
Micah 40
Nahum 41
Habakkuk 42
Zephaniah 43
Haggai 44
Zechariah 45
Malachi 46

God's Plan Continues 47

NEW TESTAMENT
Matthew 48
Mark 50
Luke 52
John 55
Acts 57
Romans 59
I Cori nthians 61
II Corinthans 62
Galatians 63
Ephesians 64
Philippians 66
Colosians 68
I Thessalonians 69
II Thessalonians 70

I Timothy............................ 72
II Timothy........................... 74
Titus................................. 75
Philemon............................ 76
Hebrews..............................77
James................................ 80
I Peter............................... 81
II Peter.............................. 82
I, II, III John........................ .84
Jude.................................. 86
Revelation........................... 89

And Now............................ 94

Bibliography........................ 95

INTRODUCTION

The Bible, God's Word,
Unique in itself,
Reveals His mind,
What we need not withheld.

His power, His glory,
His mercy, His grace,
His justice, His judgment
for mankind...their place.

The fall of mankind,
His judgment is just,
He punishes sin,
As a good judge must.

A people He chose
By which to reveal,
There's only one God,
His sovereignty real.

Again, and again,
More chances we get,
To those who repent
And their sins they regret.

His Son, He sent
To this earth to die,
On that cross, that day
For your sins and mine.

His ultimate Will
For redemption of man,
Shouts through these pages
His perfect plan.

Genesis

In the beginning
God was there,
Creating all nature
And mankind, so fair.

Characters rise,
Many names that we know,
Begins Adam and Eve,
From their story we grow.

The fall of mankind,
Satan's lies do take wing,
Judgments of sin
Through the future does ring.

Wickedness grows,
The wrath of God grave,
Noah is righteous,
As the Flood takes depraved.

The rainbow God set
In the sky as a sign,
Never again to flood
The earth by design.

God's covenant with Abraham,
For his seed and a land,
A promise forever
Is God's holy plan.

Then Isaac and Jacob
And Joseph his son,
Soon all come to Egypt
Where slavery's begun.

From Creation to man,
To world events,
Individuals and nations,
This book does present.

*In the beginning God
created the heavens and the earth.*
Genesis 1:1

Exodus

In Egypt for four hundred
Years they did slave,
Then a deliverer was born,
He was spared from the grave.

Raised by Pharaoh,
Though he was a Jew,
Moses learned about God,
And his faith quickly grew.

Escaping Hebrews,
Through the parted Red Sea,
Ten Commandments were given,
God's laws were revealed.

Rebellion prevailed,
Unbelief was their way,
Forty years in the desert,
God's decision was, stay.

To this chosen people
His will God revealed,
The Messiah will come
For redemption to seal.

> *Then Moses stretched out his hand over the sea...*
> Exodus 14:21

LEVITICUS

Learning begins
For God's will in their lives,
Worship and warnings
And rituals arrive.

Observances, conditions
Of all Holy Days,
Spiritual truths,
Of all of God's ways.

Priests and offerings,
And sacrifices for sin,
Daily holy living
For women and men.

Laws and prophesies
For the new Promised Land,
For Israel, God's chosen,
His promises will stand.

> *But if his offering is from the flock, of the sheep or of the goats, for a burnt offering, he shall offer it a male without defect.*
> Leviticus 1:10

Numbers

After forty years of wandering,
That should have been days,
They're settling and learning,
More of God's ways.

The Tabernacle was built,
God revealed His commands,
Camp order was set,
In this desert land.

A census was taken
Of all fighting men,
Building their army,
God's plan to defend.

Unbelief and rebellion
Continued to play,
Complaints were common,
Keeping the new land at bay.

This family, this people,
A nation became,
Would possess a new land,
That for them God had claimed.

> *Take a census of all the congregation of the sons of Israel…*
> Numbers 1:2

Deuteronomy

Love and obey,
The teachings are real,
Man's response to God's love,
God makes His deal.

Final instructions
For Israel's good,
From Moses, their leader;
In God's grace he stood.

Conflicts are faced
By God's chosen people,
But His love and protection
Are always faithful.

Because of the idols
Of pagan foundations,
They are to be separate
From all other nations.

Moses died
By the kiss of God,
With deliberation and care
Angels upturned the sod.

> *"You shall have no other gods before Me."*
> Deuteronomy 5:7

JOSHUA

A new leader anointed,
A new generation too,
The promised land entered,
To them, it was new.

Possession of the land,
Obedience and trust,
Faithfulness of the Covenant
With God, was a must.

Conflict and conquest
Through God's Mighty power,
At one time, the sun stopped;
God held the hour.

Jacob's sons,
The names of twelve tribes,
On this new conquered land,
The Jews now reside.

Assurance that obedience
Is rewarded by God,
But disobedience requires
Some use of the rod.

And it came to pass,
This servant of the Lord,
Joshua died,
Now receives his reward.

JUDGES

From Joshua's death
To Samuel, stood
Twelve judges that served;
Most bad, but some good.

Backsliding and falls,
Many ups and down,
Loyalty to God
Was not often found.

Deborah, Gideon,
Samson, Delilah,
Not all characters here
Lived by the law.

Failure, lawlessness,
Right in their own eyes,
Not consulting with God
For righteous advice.

Not all were bad judges;
Some tried to do right.
People are people,
Without God, it's a fight.

Ruth

The time of the judges
Is the time of this story,
Ruth, though a foreigner,
Brings to God glory.

The doctrine of redemption,
The kinsman redeemer,
Points us to Jesus,
Our future Redeemer

Genealogy lines
Lead to Christ from David,
And this little book reveals
Just what God did.

Faithfulness, godliness,
loyalty, love,
For us that's desired,
From God up above.

> *"... for where you go, I will go, and where you lodge, I will lodge. Your people shall be my people, and your God, my God."*
> Ruth 1:16

I Samuel

Judges and prophets,
And kings did arise,
In these events of history,
Though few of them wise.

Samuel's life ended,
The judges now reign,
Now, God sends prophets
To speak in His name.

Saul is anointed,
Israel's first king,
But rebellion resulted
In another's reign.

Since boyhood, David,
His God, he did love,
He slew Goliath, the giant
With help from above.

Though attempting to kill
God's next chosen king,
Protection for David
Is under God's wing.

Saul slain in battle,
Both he and his son;
Saul's heart never bowed,
from the Lord he did run.

II Samuel

David mourns
Jonathan and Saul,
He is then crowned king
Over Judah and all.

God makes a covenant
With David for plans,
For the new temple's building,
Long awaited and grand.

Triumphs of David,
Valiant in war,
Uniting all Israel,
He did this and more.

Sins he committed,
Blood on his hands,
So, by Solomon, his son,
God's temple will stand.

> *Then the men of Judah came and there anointed David king over the house of Judah.*
> 11 Samuel 2:4

I & II Kings

David as king,
Set the bar mighty high,
For each following king,
God's standard to apply.

The Northern Kingdom,
To captivity was sent,
Results of rebellion,
From Israel they went.

After one hundred
And thirty-seven years, or so,
The Southern Kingdom's taken captive,
Another blow.

The value of obedience,
The danger of not,
Can determine God's moves,
His actions, His fiat.

From these two books
The proof is in,
We can't rule the world
In our infinite sin.

Yet the Lord warned Israel and Judah,
11 Kings 17:13

I & II Chronicles

The book of Kings,
A political history,
Now, Chronicles tells
Of their religious story.

Chronicles interprets
The Book of Kings,
It helps comprehension
Of important things.

This book was written
Of their time in captivity,
In Babylon, a great
And mighty city.

But through the rough times
A remnant had hope in
That God didn't forsake them
And their chains would be broken.

> *Whoever there is among you of all His people, may the Lord his God be with him and let him go up!*
> 11 Chronicles 36:23b

Ezra

Cyrus, the king,
Declared a decree,
To rebuild God's temple
With the Jews he'd set free.

A great reformer,
And also, revivalist,
Ezra gave an account,
A quite detailed list.

Exiles return
For the temple's re-build,
They were grateful and thankful,
And rightly skilled.

Ezra, a ready
Scribe in the Law,
Desired to teach it,
To one and to all.

Ezra prayed,
Confessed and cried,
A great congregation
Confessed at his side.

He read them God's law,
They heard what was said,
A revival began,
Their hungry souls fed.

Nehemiah

The temple was built,
But the walls were in ruin,
Nehemiah would return,
Walls and gates were a shoo-in.

Opposition from within,
Ridicule and threat,
To halter this endeavor,
But God's man would not quit.

The work was finished
In fifty-two days,
Only God could have done this...
His purpose, His ways.

Some were back in the land
Post captivity,
They would hear God's Word
With great festivity.

Prayer and revival,
Reform and repentance,
The people were willing,
To God, give dependence.

> *So the wall was completed...*
> Nehemiah 6:15

Esther

God's providence and guidance,
Sometimes unseen,
By His hand for the future,
For His plans and His means.

In the shadow of this book
God directs these events,
Of His people, among pagans,
We see His footprints.

Again, Satan's scheme
Was to kill all the Jews,
But Esther,
God's chosen,
Would foil this ruse.

Satan failed again
In his supreme goal,
God again saved
His treasured fold.

> *And the letters were sent by couriers to all the king's provinces to destroy, to kill, and to annihilate all the Jews...*
> Esther 3:13a

Job

God is sovereign
And God is right,
To argue, to question
Could bring on a fight.

All people suffer,
Some righteous, some not,
From sin or just human,
Patience is taught.

Sometimes, God
Allows Satan to test
Some of His own,
Some of His best.

Job's losses were great,
He was counseled by friends,
They mourned him and judged him
For days on end.

Through his suffering and pain,
And questions and tears,
At last, he acknowledged
His pride to his peers.

Job never blamed God,
Though he wanted to die,
His faithfulness proved
That Satan does lie.

God questions Job,
"Can you do what I've done?
I have made everything,
Including the sun."

Job heard, understood,
He saw and was sorry.
God is Sovereign, all power,
Forever His glory.

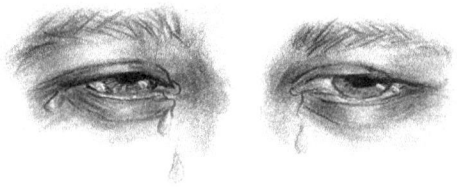

"However, put forth Thy hand, now, and touch his bone and his flesh; he will curse Thee to Thy face."
Job 2:5

Psalms

Great men of old,
Some prophets, some kings,
Poured out their hearts
About a great many things.

Their feelings and praises
And worship in song,
Are the content and essence
In these chapters of Psalms.

In Psalms, Christ is found
From birth to the cross,
Resurrection and glory,
Not one thing was lost.

Psalms blesses the soul,
It comforts the heart,
It's as good for today,
As it was at the start.

> *I have called upon Thee, for Thou wilt answer me, Oh God; Incline Thine ear to me, hear my speech.*
> Psalm 17:6

PROVERBS

Wisdom and folly,
Foolish and wise,
Many sayings, many lessons,
This book will advise.

Accolades and warnings,
Guidance and consequence,
Rules of conduct,
Just plain common sense.

A high moral plain,
This book is about,
For all to live by,
Let God's Word call you out.

> *Trust in the Lord with all your heart, and do not lean on your own understanding.*
> Proverbs 3:5

Ecclesiastes

Vanity, vanity,
King Solomon writes,
No purpose, no goal,
Just wasted lives.

His search to discover
What's good and what's true
In a life without God,
Let's emptiness brew.

He studies and lives
And learns of these things,
An endeavor of fools,
Through this book sings.

Life itself
Is not always fair,
So, trust it to God,
Our burdens, He bears.

> *Fear God and keep His commandments, because this applies to every person.*
> Ecclesiastes 12:13

Song of Solomon

Songs of love
We've heard for years,
Too many times,
End in tears.

But authentic love
Created by God,
Through marriage
By Him, is not facade.

In this book
Man's wedded love shows,
Joy and glory,
A gift that soon grows.

This book is a mirror
Of God's love of His own,
A picture of Christ
And His church, here is shown.

> *"I am my beloved's, and his desire is for me."*
> Song of Solomon 7:10

Isaiah

Prophesies, history,
Poetry, law,
From its depths, many riches,
A wise man can draw.

In the name of the Lord,
This prophet did speak,
Events of his day
And a most future "Week".

Judgments on Israel,
Sins spelled out,
Captivity lived,
Promised salvation was sought.

Of the first coming of Christ,
Many prophecies tell,
Giving hope to all captives,
Salvation from Hell.

Of the Great Tribulation
The prophet foretold,
Trouble and hardships
From the enemy of old.

In the end of times
God will make all things right,
We're exalted, remembered,
Saved by His might.

JEREMIAH

Jeremiah, a priest,
Called by the Lord,
To go in His name
Prophesying, the sword.

Because love of his people,
His heart was so broken,
But, called to this cause,
Mighty God had spoken

As sure as was told
The Babylonians came,
God's Word was fulfilled,
Fulfilled in His name.

A faithful God,
In His mercy and love,
His wrath had its limits,
Soon reprieve from above.

Again, Judah strayed,
To idols they bowed,
Judgment would come,
A very dark cloud.

> *"Before I formed you in the womb I knew you, and before you were born I consecrated you;"*
> Jeremiah 1:5

LAMENTATIONS

Poetic in form,
Comes their despair and tears,
The people of Judah
Suffered for years.

The loss of the city,
The temple and land,
Destruction of Jerusalem,
That once was so grand.

The Lord has given
To His wrath, full vent.
The cause was their sins,
They refused to repent.

"Woe to us,"
They cried, "we have sinned."
"Restore us, Oh God,
On You we depend.

Because of God's love
They were not consumed,
For His compassion won't fail,
Hope always blooms.

> *The punishment of your iniquity has been completed, O daughter of Zion;*
> Lamentations 4:22

Ezekiel

An exile in Babylon,
Ezekiel was called,
To confront God's people
About sins of them all.

His vision was crucial,
The message was clear,
To become a watchman,
My words you shall hear.

Speak to the Israelites,
Warn them from Me,
Turn from your ways
And from all evil flee.

The warning to Judah,
Was Ezekiel's task, They
defiled themselves With
despicable acts.

The God of compassion
Forgets not His chosen,
Restored in the future,
They can have hope in.

Many nations are judged,
His clear vision shows,
All were fulfilled,
Our Mighty God knows.

Tomorrow is God's,
But to Ezekiel reveals,
What all will happen then,
In the future, is sealed.

The hope for the people,
The temple restored,
In many days' future,
Peace from the Lord.

> *Then He said to me, "Son of man, I am sending you to the sons of Israel, to a rebellious people who have rebelled against Me..."*
> Ezekiel 2:3a

Daniel

Daniel and friends,
To captivity taken,
To serve the King,
But from God, not forsaken.

To these men,
God gave Knowledge and learning,
And to Daniel, He gave
Visions of dreams, discerning.

Dreams of the king,
No sorcerer could tell,
God's answers to Daniel
Were clear as a bell.

To convince Jewish exiles,
God is still Sovereign,
Visions of end times,
And how redemption is gotten.

The peak of God's Sovereignty
In Revelation is shown,
Destinies of nations
And Israel's are known.

> *However, there is a God in heaven who reveals mysteries,*
> Daniel 2:28

Hosea

Hosea, a prophet
Of times that were spoken,
In tragic days lived,
Northern kingdom falls broken.

A faithful husband,
But his wife was untrue,
Mirrors God's faithfulness,
But Israel's faithlessness too.

Israel's punishment,
Judgment pronounced,
God's wrath poured out,
But sins weren't renounced.

Their sins were many,
Their hostility great,
The corruption was deep,
God knew their fate.

Still God is faithful,
His ways are profound,
"Return and repent",
His blessings abound.

> *Come let us return to the Lord. For He has torn us, but He will heal us;*
> Hosea 6:1

JOEL

The Great and Terrible
Day of the Lord,
Brings judgment and wrath,
Along with the sword.

A call to mourning,
Repentance and prayer,
Rend your heart, while you can,
Those days none can bear.

Near is the Day
God's destruction will come,
Don't test the Lord,
His will… will be done.

Nations are anguished
As faces turn pale,
This display of God's power,
Which cannot fail.

God remembers His people,
though earth's nations are judged.
He blesses His people;
He won't hold a grudge.

> *Alas for the day! For the day of the Lord is near, and it will come as destruction from the Almighty.*
> Joel 1:15

Amos

What Amos saw
Two years prior,
Israel's neighbors
Being judged, God brings fire.

To God's chosen people,
Oracles spoken,
About social injustice,
All laws have been broken.

Complacent and prideful,
They angered the Lord,
He called them to seek Him,
Or face the sword.

But God, in His mercy
Gives hope to His own,
The future day's coming,
Endless joy will be known.

> *"So I will send fire upon the house of Hazael, and it will consume the citadels of Ben-hadad."*
> Amos 1:4

Obadiah

In a vision, the Lord
Made known to this man,
A Word of destruction
Was soon in God's plan.

Edom, the prideful,
Dared to mock God.
By joining in violence
Of their brothers, with a nod.

They turned on their brothers,
Boasting of their misfortune,
"It will be done to you,
What you have done.", is their fortune.

But Israel's deliverance
By God in His mercy,
They will possess the land
In complete victory.

> *The vision of Obadiah.*
> *Thus says the Lord God*
> *concerning Edom-*
> Obadiah 1:1

JONAH

Sent by God to Nineveh,
A city of wickedness,
Jonah rebelled and escaped
God's command he suppressed.

A storm risked the ship,
Jonah thrown over,
A great fish swallowed him,
Prayer for help, got him sober.

Humbled and freed,
To Nineveh he journeyed,
To proclaim God's Word,
God interceded.

A lesson from God,
Lost people He loves,
Don't run if you're called,
God finds you, He does.

> *And the Lord appointed a great fish to swallow Jonah, and Jonah was in the stomach of the fish three days and three nights.*
> Jonah 1:17

MICAH

Micah, God's prophet,
Receives the Word,
Against Samaria, and Jerusalem,
Their sins, too absurd.

Warns of false prophets,
Speaking ungodly lies,
But promises deliverance,
In time will arrive.

It tells of the Last Days,
The Lord's Holy plans,
The promised Messiah
Will come to this land.

Act justly, walk humbly,
Love the mercy of God,
His anger will cease,
He'll withhold, the rod.

Who is like God,
Who pardons sins,
Of the remnant, His people,
His inheritance.

> *For behold, the Lord is coming*
> *forth from His place.*
> Micah 1:3

Nahum

Built on wickedness and tyranny,
Such a kingdom must fall,
For evil plots against God,
Nahum is called.

Once in revival,
Back to paganism, returned,
God's judgment is righteous,
Through their sin, they have earned.

> *Whatever you devise against the Lord, He will make a complete end of it. Distress will not rise up twice.*
> Nahum 1:9

Habakkuk

Why is there evil,
Injustice and strife?
Why are wrongs and violence,
Allowed in this life?

Habakkuk pleaded,
Habakkuk prayed,
God's answers will come,
But judgment is made.

The Lord's in His temple,
Be silent before Him.
He is my strength, praise to God,
I am filled to the brim.

> *Why art Thou silent when the wicked swallowed up those more righteous than they?*
> Habakkuk 1:13b

ZEPHANIAH

Judgment, seems
The dark side of God's love,
But it can motivate repentance,
Then forgiveness, thereof.

Warnings of end times,
Great fear of God's wrath,
His righteous anger
Will soon come to pass.

But God is all faithful
In mercy and care,
Restoration is promised,
We have hope to share.

> *Near is the great day of the*
> *Lord, near and*
> *coming very quickly;*
> Zephaniah 1:14

Haggai

God sent a message
To the prophet, Haggai,
Rebuild the temple...
Too much time has gone by.

God said, "Be strong,"
To the people of the land,
Tomorrow's blessing
Will be at hand.

> *"Go up to the mountains, bring wood and rebuild the temple, that I may be pleased with it and be glorified."* says the Lord.
> Haggai 1:8

Zechariah

Don't...repeat
Your father's sins,
Return to Me,
For on Me all depends.

In one night alone
Ten visions, he saw,
Scenes of the last days,
The prophet's in awe.

Of Jesus, Messiah,
Oracles spoken,
End time events,
Of nations and His chosen.

> *"Sing for joy and be glad, O daughter of Zion; for behold I am coming and I will dwell in your midst,"* declares the Lord.
> Zechariah 2:10

Malachi

God again declares
His love for His people,
But contempt for His name
By their actions was guileful.

The Day of the Lord
Is coming…, it's dire,
The evil will burn,
They'll succumb to God's fire.

> *"A son honors his father, and a servant his master. Then if I am a Father, where is My honor? And if I am a Master, where is My respect?" says the Lord of hosts to you, O priests who despise My name?"*
> Malachi 1:6

God's Plan Continues, His Mystery Unfolds

At the end of Old Testament,
Four hundred years passed,
The coming of Jesus,
The New Testament cast.

The new hope of many,
God's plan is revealed,
Jesus' death on the cross,
Our salvation is sealed.

Read on expectantly,
Open your heart,
Let God show His wonders,
Matthew's the start.

Matthew

Written in Greek,
Matthew writes to the Jews,
The world ruler is Rome,
And he brings the good news.

New Testament opens,
Genealogy of Christ,
Proves that Jesus, Messiah,
Is the new Sacrifice.

Pharisees, Sadducees,
Herodians and Scribes,
Different parties we meet,
Here, Matthew describes.

The Baptist, the wise men,
The Virgin and more,
Jesus' birth, early life,
Set the tone, the ground floor.

The ministry of Christ
To these people was new,
He performed teaching and miracles,
All in plain view.

Matthew presents
Christ, Messiah and King,
But, the religious, the nation,
To their traditions did cling.

Matthew writes
Of Christ's death on the cross,
His sacrifice made,
To save the lost.

Jesus, the King
And Lord of Lords,
In Him, only,
Salvation is born.

> *The book of the
> genealogy of
> Jesus Christ,
> the Son of David,
> the Son of Abraham.*
> Matthew 1:1

Mark

The gospel of Mark
Is brief and blunt,
He gets right to the point,
With great action out front.

In Mark's gospel he shows
Christ as servant,
He writes to the strongman,
To the Romans, the fervent.

Again, is the gospel,
The good news of God,
Forgiveness of sins
To the people, seemed odd.

Miracles of Christ
Put the people in awe,
Mark established with proof,
Christ the Messiah.

Christ had authority
Over demons, He proved,
This confused many people,
Some believed, some refused.

Calming the storm,
Walking on water,
Casting out demons,
From the dead, raised a daughter.

Parables spoken,
Explaining His teachings,
He taught God's will,
To all, hopefully reaching.

The plot to kill Jesus,
The betrayal exposed,
Satan's plan moving swiftly,
His plan is imposed.

Jesus hung on that cross,
They thought in defeat,
Three days later He rose,
God's plan was complete.

Five hundred folks,
Eye witnesses, you see,
Risen, ascended,
Back to heaven, victory.

LUKE

A learned physician,
Historian and poet,
More truth of Jesus,
He succeeds, to unfold it.

Jesus, the perfect,
Divine, man and Savior,
God, manifested in flesh
Shown as the Creator.

Fulfilling the prophecy,
A messenger was born,
"Repent of your sins,
Prepare for the Lord."

The forerunner of Christ
Was the Baptist, John,
To announce the Lord's coming,
Their salvation had come.

The birth of Jesus,
His early life,
Satan's temptations,
Caused his hunger and strife.

His ministry starts,
He's rejected at home,
He travels, and preaches,
His Word becomes known.

*And it came about that while
He was blessing them,
He parted from them.*
Luke 24:51

JOHN

The most profound gospel,
John excels in this book,
The depths of holy mysteries,
He dares you to look.

Showing Christ as God's Son,
The Word made Flesh,
Eternal life's provider,
Our souls to refresh.

Written to believers
For the purpose of growth,
The treasures and mysteries,
The God/Man, He's both.

This gospel records
Seven times Christ is seen,
After rising from death,
More proof is gleaned.

The deity of Christ
Is emphasized here,
Mindful of His wonders,
There's nothing to fear.

Fearful and angry,
His enemies became,
Diabolical schemes,
And Jesus was slain.

From eternity past,
He came to reveal,
His gift of salvation,
At His name all will kneel.

Assuming victory,
Accomplishing their goal,
But He rose from the grave
In complete control.

He blessed His disciples
And he rose in the clouds,
In joy, they worshiped
And praised Him aloud.

> *In the beginning was the Word,*
> *and the Word was with God,*
> *and the Word was God.*
> *And the Word became flesh,*
> *and dwelt among us.*
> John 1:1,14

Acts

Christian origins
And the spread of the gospel
Of Jesus' life and His teachings
Were taken to all.

Jesus had told them,
The disciples, I mean,
Wait for My Spirit,
On His guidance you'll lean.

At the time of the feasts
To Jerusalem they journeyed,
In one place they gathered
For God to proceed.

Suddenly, then,
Like a violent wind,
Like tongues of fire,
The Holy Spirit descends.

Now, filled with God's power
Their missions began,
Many miles traveled,
Sharing the gospel, to man

Persecution and prison
Most disciples endured.
The first martyr was Stephen,
His end was severe.

The conversion of Saul,
The Pharisee, cruel,
Confronted by Jesus,
Saul, no longer a fool.

By the Spirit of God,
Saul became Paul,
A major disciple,
He'd received his call.

Through these disciples,
Ordinary men,
Came God's faithful proclaimers,
The Church did begin.

> *And suddenly there came from heaven a noise like a violent, rushing wind, and it filled the whole house where they were sitting. And there appeared to them tongues as of fire...*
> Acts 2:2, 3a

Romans

A manifesto for the world,
Now Gentiles included,
The first church in Rome,
No one excluded.

A great theme of this book,
The righteousness of God,
God's plan of salvation
Clearing any facade.

Paul illustrates law,
Faith, and right living,
Some hard to hear,
Being sinners and slipping.

Not many admit
That all people sin,
Or a Holy God sees it,
And it hurts Him within.

Justified by faith
On the merit of Christ,
Is new to so many,
But in truth, this abides.

Spiritual gifts
To believers are given,
Through His grace, and love,
powerful lives we can live in.

The promise to Israel
That God one time gave,
Is fulfilled in the future,
The Jews will be saved.

Daily life rules,
By Paul, are written,
To help us live holy,
Like Christ, the Risen.

New heaven, new earth,
A reality soon,
In God's timing, His purpose,
The end of all gloom.

Face life with these books,
Let them be your guide,
From today till forever,
In heaven we'll abide.

For all have sinned and fall short of the glory of God,
Romans 3:23

I Corinthians

Epistles were letters
To believers in Corinth,
To address different subjects
And problems within.

This place was known
For its debauchery and drunkenness,
Against such corruption,
Paul is teaching God's holiness.

Impurity, lawsuits,
Marriage and dress,
Liberty, communion
And spiritual gifts.

With passion, Paul addressed
All of these things,
God's people He's raising
To be kids of the King

> *Brethren, do not be children in your thinking; yet in evil be babes, but in your thinking be mature.*
> 1Corinthians 14:20

II Corinthians

Attacked by false teachers,
Accused of such lies,
Paul defends his actions,
Teaches forgiveness, all wise.

Seeing the Glory of God
With unveiled faces,
Is the promise to believers,
To God, all our praises.

The prospect of death,
What it means for Christians,
Life eternal, new bodies,
And no more questions.

The principle here
Of righteous giving,
Generosity encouraged,
To help the poor's living.

Examine ourselves,
Is Paul's final warning,
Have we faith, or not?
Know yourself, start exploring.

> *Test yourself to see if you are in the faith;*
> *examine yourselves!*
> 11 Corinthians 13:5a

GALATIANS

A fighting epistle
At this time was needed,
Legalism verses liberty,
For clarity Paul pleaded.

This strong declaration
And defense of this doctrine,
Justification by faith,
From this we can't run.

Saved by faith
But living by law,
Perpetrates falling,
From grace, it's a flaw.

Given by Moses,
The Law for that time,
But grace came by Jesus,
To ignore this, a crime.

We're called to bear
One another's burdens,
For by this, Christians grow,
This, we have learned of.

Ephesians

Expanding the horizons
Of Paul's readers,
Teaching depths of God's grace
To new believers.

The church is a body
By God, it was planned,
God's Son paid its price,
Holy Spirit, makes it stand.

A mystery, the church,
Its origin, Christ,
Sharing Christ's promise,
Jews and Gentiles alike.

Gentle and humble
We are called to live,
Unity, and love
To one another, to give.

God has an order
For heaven and home,
To keep us from chaos,
Going off on our own.

The Spiritual Armor,
Is the Armor of God,
It protects from the dark worlds,
The Devil's rod.

*Put on the full Armor of God,
that you may be able to stand
firm against the schemes
of the devil.*
Ephesians 6:11

Philippians

Another letter
Written from jail.
Tender love he sends,
Somehow, by some mail.

To God, working in them,
Grateful is Paul,
Knowing, he'll continue His work
Till Jesus comes to all.

The entire way
Of conducting our life,
Should be credit to the gospel,
That's in praise of Christ.

Beware of evil,
Rejoice in the Lord,
Trusting our flesh,
We just can't afford.

Righteousness comes
Through faith in Christ,
Not of our own,
Because He paid the price.

For believers, our citizenship
Is in heaven.
We eagerly wait,
Our Savior, leaves no question.

*Only conduct yourselves in a
manner worthy of the
gospel of Christ;*
Philippians 1:27a

Colossians

Still in prison,
To Colossians, Paul sends
This letter concerning
The heresy, to end.

Paul prays for knowledge
For the brethren, in faith,
Walk worthy, with wisdom,
Be fruitful and gain.

It pleased God to give
All fullness, to Christ,
Making peace through His blood,
The cross was the price.

Beware of trust
In philosophy and deceit,
Man's wisdom will only
Lead to defeat.

We are to seek those things
From God above,
Our hope is coming,
The Savior of Love.

I Thessalonians

Encouraging words,
As father to son,
Paul supports young converts,
Their new lives' begun.

It is God's will
That you be sanctified,
Avoid immoral acts,
The Holy Spirit's your guide.

Important prophetic
Passages here,
It's imminent and impending,
Christ will appear.

His own, He will take,
From this world soon one day,
Be joyful, rejoice,
Give thanks and pray.

At the trumpet call
The dead will rise,
Caught up, and alive,
We'll gaze in His eyes.

> *The Lord Himself will descend
> from heaven with a shout,*
> 1 Thessalonians 4:16

II Thessalonians

With a false report
That Christ had returned,
Paul sends this letter
To calm fears of concern.

Perseverance and faith
This church endured,
God is Just in their suffering,
His vengeance assured.

This Word of God
Makes it quite clear,
In this life will be trouble,
Trust, do not to fear.

That Day will come
After rebellion takes place,
That man of lawlessness
States his case.

Satan will empower,
This Anti-Christ!
Stand firm, God's plan
We know will suffice.

Hold to the teachings
You know to be true,
Of doing right, never tire,
God stands with you.

Let no one in any way deceive you, for it will not come unless the apostacy comes first, and the man of lawlessness is revealed, the son of destruction,
11 Thessalonians 2:3

I Timothy

False doctrines were taught
Confusing believers,
Heresy in the church
From clever deceivers.

God, in His Will
Gave instructions on worship,
For praying women and men,
What the church shall permit.

Of the church officers,
The character and life,
Is utmost important,
And, just having one wife.

Self-controlled, temperate,
And also, be kind,
Respectable, hospitable,
With God's Word aligned.

Instructions to Timothy
About latter days,
False teachings come;
Some depart from the faith.

Instructing him, dealing with
All groups in the fold,
Practical info
For church order to hold.

Love of money, false teachers
And arrogance in wealth,
Timothy warns about these,
For the church health.

...In order that you may instruct certain men not to teach strange doctrines, nor to pay attention to myths and endless genealogies, which give rise to mere speculation rather than furthering the administration of God which is by faith.
1 Timothy 1:3b, 4

II Timothy

Paul exhorts Timothy
To be strong in grace,
The grace that's in Jesus,
Our only firm base.

Warn the people
Against quarreling with words,
It's of no value
And those listening, it hurts.

Again, warning of apostasy
In the last days,
Rampant evil, corruption,
Unholy, their ways.

In these latter days
God's Word we're to preach,
Keeping the faith,
The world we're to reach.

... of Jesus Christ, who is to judge the living and the dead, and by His appearing and His kingdom: preach the Word.
11 Timothy 4:1,2a

Titus

Essential, instructions
For the church to survive,
With good officials, good teaching,
True humility, derives.

Last, but not least,
A word to the wise,
Commit to what's right
Is good in God's eyes.

> *Remind them to be subject to rulers, to authorities, to be obedient, to be ready for every good deed, to malign no one, to be uncontentious, gentle, showing every consideration for all men.*
> Titus 3:1,2

PHILEMON

Philemon lived
In a place called Colossae,
An owner of slaves,
But not a bad guy.

He ran from his owner,
Onesimus, a slave,
Met Paul, while in prison,
And the gospel, Paul gave.

Paul sends him home
To Philemon with a plea,
As a brother in Christ
Accept him as you do me.

> *I appeal to you for my child,
> whom I've begotten in my
> imprisonment, Onesimus,*
> Philemon 1:10

Hebrews

This letter assures
That the Law is still good,
But that grace, under Christ
Must be understood.

Of angels, and prophets,
And forefathers, too,
God's Son is superior,
Jesus is Who.

Higher than angels,
His deity shown,
But still, full human,
He stepped down from the throne.

As our High Priest,
Christ, is God's final Word.
Through Him, it's written,
God's way is heard.

It's now time to grow
In the one true faith,
Continued falling, and sinning,
Is a slap in Christ's face.

God is just,
And Christ knows who are His,
This is His promise,
Our righteous God says.

Putting laws in their minds
And written on their hearts,
This New Covenant with Israel,
In the last days, will start.

Sacrificing animals,
Sins forgiven for a year,
Now, one sacrifice of Christ,
Man's sins, ever clear.

The faith chapter, eleven,
Is known throughout,
Faith connects you to God,
That's what it's about.

Coming to God
By faith, is the way,
Or, it's impossible to please Him,
Scripture, does say.

Discipline's part
Of God's way with His own,
Like a parent who cares,
This has been shown.

Give thanks to the Lord,
It's the right thing to do,
For all His great blessings
Are precious and true.

Since then we have a great high priest who has passed through the heavens, Jesus the Son of God, let us hold fast our confession.
               Hebrews 4:14

JAMES

Are we tested by God?
Yes, we are, sometimes.
Through trials, His Word,
But not evil, divine.

Warned against worldliness,
It's not to pursue,
It leads to conflict,
Leaves God out of view.

In concerns of this life,
Don't run from our God;
Fall at His feet,
Be spared from the rod.

> *Blessed is a man who perseveres under trial; for once he has been approved, He will receive the crown of life, which the Lord has promised to those who love Him.*
> James 1:12

I Peter

Doctrines of God
That are covered here,
Teach the reader God's Word,
Peter makes clear.

Calling all Christians
In living, be holy,
Be separate to God
With attitudes, lowly.

Know the Bible,
Cause that way you'll see,
When folks come with questions,
Prepared, you will be.

We're told to give
An answer to all,
For the reason we hope,
That is our call.

> *Sanctify Christ as Lord in your hearts, always being ready to make a defense to everyone who asks you to give an account for the hope that is in you, yet with gentleness and reverence.*
> 1 Peter 3:15

II Peter

Final words of Peter,
Before breathing his last,
Warns believers, heed his words,
Make this your task.

Prophecies in Scripture
Were spoken by God,
Not man's interpretation,
Insuring no fraud.

The pull of the world
Away from our God,
Apostacy, despair,
Indifference abroad.

False teachers and teachings,
Enticing man,
Shameful and demeaning,
All over, will fan.

There is coming real soon
Scoffers of truth,
Ignorance, and disbelief,
From Satan, on cue.

Grow in knowledge,
In the grace of our Lord,
Be on guard,
Don't let His Word be ignored

But false prophets also rose among the people, just as there will also be false teachers among you,
11 Peter 2:1a

I, II, III John

We're to walk in the light,
For God is Light,
Run from the darkness,
Fight the good fight.

Do not entertain
Or believe every spirit,
Are they from God?
Test their merit!

Children of God
Are those who believe,
That His Son, Christ Jesus,
To His commandments, we cleave.

Forgiveness is given
To those who repent,
For our sins were placed on
The One whom God sent.

Know that you know,
Eternal life is to be,
Trust in Christ Jesus,
The Savior, is He.

Love one another,
For this is God's way,
Pray and obey,
In His will you need stay.

Beloved, do not believe every spirit, but test the spirits to see whether they are from God; because many false prophets have gone out into the world.
1 John 4:1

Jude

Believers, for faith
Earnestly strive.
Once for all, delivered,
For the spiritually alive.

Thousands of holy ones
Coming with Christ,
To judge, to convict,
Evil deeds, despised.

More mockers they'll be
In the last days,
Their own lust they follow,
Trusting in their own ways.

But believers in Christ,
In faith, stay strong,
Waiting the mercy of Christ,
Is where we belong.

In mercy,
Some will be snatched from the fire,
Some have mercy through fear,
Eternal life to acquire.

To Him who is able
To keep you from falling,
May we stand in His presence,
Worthy of His calling.

"In the last time there shall be mockers, following after their own ungodly lusts".
Jude 1:18

Revelation

To persecuted Christians
This letter brings hope,
Providing a vision,
Big, in anyone's scope.

God knows the past,
The present and future,
This time that is coming,
We can know, and be sure.

A prophetic book
To this world has been given,
The Creator has spoken,
Come awake, pay attention.

Systematic events
Symbolically told,
Ultimate horrors
The world will behold.

This Great Tribulation
So long ago seen,
Evil is present,
Satan's diabolical scheme.

A tyrant, coming ruler,
With a fierce iron rod,
In the temple he'll stand
And he'll claim to be God.

Each plague, each trouble,
Each death is a call,
People, oh, people,
Repent, one and all.

Hard hearted people,
Rebellious in pride,
Fearful and suffering,
Earth's people cried.

A mark of this beast
Must be taken by all,
Or, buy not, nor sell not,
Nor live not…his law.

For seven years
With death and destruction,
Hopeless, in bondage
Is the world's situation.

Opens, heaven,
And behold a white horse,
Upon him a rider,
With justice, makes war.

Faithful and True,
From His mouth comes a sword,
He's the Word of God,
King of Kings, Lord of Lords.

In the lake of fire,
The tyrants are thrown,
And those with Antichrist's mark
It's no longer postponed.

After a thousand years
It's now Satan's doom,
The judgment of all,
And the new world blooms.

I'm the Alpha, Omega,
Beginning and End,
Now, God reconciles
Man as His friend.

We've been given the warnings,
Don't let them slip by,
Come, Lord Jesus,
Our waiting hearts cry.

> *"I am the Alpha and the Omega, the First and the Last, the Beginning and the End."*
> Revelation 22:13

And now...

Now that you have gotten a glimpse of what the Bible has to offer, as you learned about some of the people, events and even some principles of the Bible.

I pray that you will be encouraged to embark on your own journey in reading the whole Word of God. Discover for yourself, the rich history, the interesting people, exciting, and at times, terrifying events. Learn how God leads people, teaches people, and cares for them.

The Bible is the one Book that can and does address all aspects of human life; it tells of our struggles, our sorrows, our joys, all of which are common to man. It reveals God's wisdom, God's power, His mercy, His offer of forgiveness for all, and His great and mighty love. You will discover His Will for mankind, and you will bow at His awesome, and righteous character.

As you read and study the Bible, you will read about prophecies, and then see how they came to pass just they were prophesied. You will learn of the last few prophecies that still remain unfulfilled, because they are still in our future.

The Bible is God's love letter to us. Read it with expectation of wonder. Welcome to the supernatural.

Bibliography

Page 10: "He died by the kiss of God."
Commentary by J. Vernon McGee
Through the Bible, by J. Vernon McGee

Page 10: "For the angels of God upturned the sod,"
Poem by Cecil Frances Alexander
"The Burial of Moses"

www.ingramcontent.com/pod-product-compliance
Lightning Source LLC
Chambersburg PA
CBHW041326110526

44592CB00021B/2833